Today God
Wants You To
Know. . .
*You Are
Beautiful*

Today God
Wants You To
Know. . .
You Are
Beautiful

Valorie Quesenberry

BARBOUR BOOKS
An Imprint of Barbour Publishing, Inc.

© 2017 by Barbour Publishing, Inc.

Print ISBN 978-1-68322-257-6

Published by Barbour Books, an imprint of Barbour Publishing, Inc., P.O. Box 719, Uhrichsville, Ohio 44683, www.barbourbooks.com

Our mission is to publish and distribute inspirational products offering exceptional value and biblical encouragement to the masses.

Member of the
Evangelical Christian
Publishers Association

Printed in the United States of America.

Contents

You are beautiful.

This book is filled with all the reasons why.

They are not entries from a positive-thinking workbook but statements of fact; truths that you can count on.

Every woman longs for beauty—in herself and in her world. That's the way God made us, crafted in His glorious image and endowed with His sensitivities and longings. Though we are a kaleidoscope of personalities, styles, and preferences, women by design have an innate knowledge that we are made for beauty.

And you, today, at this moment, reflect an unspeakable beauty.

God sees it. He wants you to believe it.

Today, He holds out His mirror to show you the woman He sees.

Today, He offers to re-energize your beauty with His redemption and healing and grace.

Today, He rejoices over you.

Go ahead; dare to believe it. Today, God wants you to know you are beautiful.

BEAUTIFUL BY DESIGN

Fabulous You

*My frame was not hidden from You
when I was being formed in secret [and]
intricately and curiously wrought [as if embroidered
with various colors] in the depths of the earth
[a region of darkness and mystery].*
PSALM 139:15 AMPC

You were made according to a pattern. No random fusion of DNA brought you into this world. Your parents may or may not have "planned" your creation, but God did. And while the little embryo that you once were was forming in that hidden place, God watched and waited until His masterpiece was ready to enter the outside world. And when the moment arrived, He knew you were beautiful. And you still are.

Amazing Thoughts

*"But there is a spirit in man, and the breath
of the Almighty gives him understanding."*

JOB 32:8 NKJV

You are beautiful from the inside out.

You were designed to radiate beauty from your very core. Often, we feel our opinions and perspective aren't significant. You may express your view and others keep right on talking. You may tell a joke and not get laughter. You may have a great idea that is ignored. But God listens to every nuance of your mind and is delighted with the person He created. To Him, you are brilliant and interesting.

Ebb and Flow

*You chart the path ahead of me and tell
me where to stop and rest. Every moment
you know where I am. You know what I
am going to say before I even say it.*

PSALM 139:3–4 TLB

God understands you. Your thoughts. Your emotions.
Your longings. What prompts them. He is intimately
acquainted with all your ways. He knows how you ride
the wave of feeling and that sometimes you sense you're
going under the crest instead of over. But He wants you
to believe that He sees beauty in the depth of you and
that no tide of emotion can drown it.

Not Found on Pinterest

*"And to one he gave five talents,
to another two, and to another one,
to each according to his own ability."*

MATTHEW 25:15 NKJV

One of a kind. That's you. With one-of-a-kind creativity.

Many women say, "I'm not creative." Not true.

Of course, it's easy to see why we would feel that way with Pinterest boards that show us all the wonderful things we could do in our spare time, and then with our friends' Facebook posts that show us "everyone else" actually doing them!

But you have unique creativity given from God. Believe that today!

A Beauty of Blessing

*There are diversities of gifts, but the same
Spirit. There are differences of ministries,
but the same Lord. And there are diversities
of activities, but it is the same God who works
all in all. But the manifestation of the Spirit
is given to each one for the profit of all.*

1 CORINTHIANS 12:4–7 NKJV

God gave you a gift in addition to your salvation.

You have been gifted with a spiritual ability, a
blessing to bring to the body of Christ. Look for it.
Discover the beautiful offering of service that is uniquely
yours to give.

Birthday Suited

But God gives to it the body that
He plans and sees fit, and to each
kind of seed a body of its own.

1 CORINTHIANS 15:38 AMPC

Apple or pear? Top-heavy, bottom-heavy, or stick-figured?

Oh, we women labor under these vivid illustrations of our bodies! And we feel shamed for our DNA-imprinted shape, which we didn't choose.

Girlfriend, you aren't responsible for the bones. Only the meat on them. The basic structure was chosen by God, and the seed that is the real you is most important anyway.

Love it and go with it! Beautify your world!

Beautiful Plan

*But from the beginning of the creation
God made them male and female.*

MARK 10:6 KJV

The idea of two distinct genders and their relationship to each other is a beautiful one. It was God's.

He designed male and female to reflect His glorious image in their complementary, covenantal relationship.

You are a specific example of this magnificent plan.

Today, embrace your beautiful femininity and express it graciously and wholesomely. Be a model of God's greatness.

He Crunches Those Numbers

*"And he knows the number
of hairs on your head!"*

LUKE 12:7 TLB

Hair.

What that word represents to a woman is hard to fathom. It is deeply linked with her identity and her beauty. God designed it that way. Yet the inventory we have to work with is fluid, and God knows the exact number you are working with today. He sees strand #3984 dangling and about to fall to the floor. He is both the giver and the keeper of your hair. And you're beautiful to Him no matter the count today!

Digits by Design

For You did form my inward parts; You did knit me together in my mother's womb.

PSALM 139:13 AMPC

I wonder how many of us actually like our fingers and toes.

Personally, I never have cared for mine. I wanted slender, tapered fingers and toes that decreased gradually in length. Alas, it was not to be. But still, our Creator has designed us to fulfill His plan, and He has given us the fingers and toes to accomplish it.

Today, marvel at the function of your digits, no matter their shape.

More Than Skin Deep

So it was, when Abram came into Egypt,
that the Egyptians saw the woman,
that she was very beautiful.

GENESIS 12:14 NKJV

We know Sarah was beautiful. But she was a woman who was beautiful while living in a desert land, exposed to harsh sun, blowing winds, and a nomadic lifestyle. And skin keeps no secrets.

Today, God says you are beautiful despite what your skin says to others. He sees the beauty that goes beyond "skin deep." He sees the spirit, which is preserved and made forever young by His grace.

The Eyes Have It

*"How beautiful you are, my love,
how beautiful! Your eyes are soft as doves'."*
SONG OF SOLOMON 1:15 TLB

The eye is the lamp of the body.
MATTHEW 6:22 AMPC

We all want beautiful eyes. And there is no shortage of tips on how to make the most of them. But, regardless of the color or size or depth of the ones you have, they are beautiful because God picked them for you.

Go look at your eyes. Everything about them says He designed you specifically for His glory. Let His light make them beautiful today.

Beautifully Disabled

*Who makes the dumb, or the deaf, or the seeing,
or the blind? Is it not I, the Lord?*

EXODUS 4:11 AMPC

Cerebral palsy. Blindness. Deafness. Autism.

These are just a few of the disabilities that are part of the human story, perhaps your story. Part of your beauty.

We think of beauty only in classical, symmetrical, sculptured terms. But beauty can be painful, ill shapen, and random. Anything the Creator has allowed to pull you closer to Him is a thing of beauty.

Today, let your defects become a reason to glory in His power.

Created for Creativity

She makes linen garments and sells them,
and supplies sashes for the merchants.

PROVERBS 31:24 NKJV

Having a home business is commended in the Bible. The Proverbs 31 woman was very definitely involved in the keeping and nurturing of her home, but she also had some business ventures going. One of them was creating beautiful items of clothing to sell to the merchants for their shops.

Using your God-given talents as an investment or to help meet the needs of your family can be a blessing. Beauty is creatively using your gifts for good.

Made for Diligence

She watches over the ways of her household,
and does not eat the bread of idleness.

PROVERBS 31:27 NKJV

God thinks you are beautiful when you are fulfilling your role. Slothfulness is a blight on beauty; industriousness is a sign of inward character, and it is beautiful.

In the animal kingdom the female species is often working to provide for her family's food. Many times, the female is the huntress. She rarely sits around idle.

While we are not identical to the animals, we are created to watch over our households. Today, be diligent. It's a sign of beauty.

BEAUTIFUL BY NATURE

Quirkily Lovely

*For He knows our frame,
He [earnestly] remembers and imprints
[on His heart] that we are dust.*
PSALM 103:14 AMPC

Just a handful of dust. That's you. But beautiful dust, because the Creator chose and formed it and imbued it with His own breath.

Dust has its lowly attributes. And you have yours. Your family, friends, and coworkers know them well, those oddities of your personality that make them raise an eyebrow or stifle a chuckle.

Maybe He smiles, too, but always with eyes of love. Those quirks identify our unique beauty.

Moods Are Not You

My tears have been my food day and night.

PSALM 42:3 AMPC

Been there?

Moods are part of our humanity and, even more specifically, part of our femaleness. Maybe your mood is hormonally based, or maybe it is caused by your grief over a prodigal child, strained marriage, or broken friendship. Maybe you've recently moved or acquired a negative diagnosis or lost a job.

Remember that He is God of our moods also, even when we don't understand them. Today, He sees the beauty in you that passing moods cannot mar.

Tempered Traits

*"I knew you before you were formed
within your mother's womb; before you
were born I sanctified you and appointed
you as my spokesman to the world."*

JEREMIAH 1:5 TLB

To what has God appointed you?

For Jeremiah, it was prophetic proclamation, and God gave him the temperament he needed for that mission.

Which temperament are you—sanguine, choleric, melancholy, phlegmatic? Which blend of inborn traits fits you for the lifework to which you are ordained?

Whatever the answer, it is part of your beauty . . .if it is surrendered to God and controlled by His Spirit.

Faves and Raves

I delight to do Your will, O my God.
PSALM 40:8 NKJV

Every one of us has a few favorite things, to quote the inimitable Julie Andrews. Rather than bright copper kettles, yours might be centered around coffee flavors, shoes, and lotions. We have favorite restaurants and events and holidays.

The psalmist said that his delight was an action. Put in a modern context, his delight was not just an Instagram photo of someone else's action; he delighted in *doing* God's will. Today, take a fresh look at God's law and then act on it. Let it become your new fave.

Celebrating You

Her clothing is fine linen and purple.
PROVERBS 31:22 NKJV

Yeah, girlfriend, you have style. Your own. The way you put together your colors and patterns and textures and accessories. You have a unique way of wearing your beauty.

God gave that to you. He put inside you a brand that only you can express. Of course, that doesn't mean He is glorified by weirdness or sloppiness or dirtiness or seductiveness. But when we steward our beauty well, He looks good and so do we.

Today, celebrate your style by honoring Him.

Love for Beauty

She makes tapestry for herself;
her clothing is fine linen and purple.
PROVERBS 31:22 NKJV

We don't know for sure just when women started caring about clothes. But a yearning for pretty clothing seems to be written on the very DNA of women.

The woman commended by God in Proverbs 31 wore fine clothing, made well and of the best color (purple was a luxury in that time).

God wants you to be beautiful by caring for yourself in the best manner you can. Honor His gift of femininity.

Beautifully Outfitted

*Strength and honor are her clothing;
she shall rejoice in time to come.*

PROVERBS 31:25 NKJV

Speaking of clothing. . .the beautiful woman of God has two items in her closet. Strength and honor. They are her basic wardrobe pieces, her essentials. She may accessorize with other things, but she is never without these.

They originate with God. He is the source of strength and the way to honor. Putting Him in first place ensures that these pieces of clothing are just your size.

And you will rejoice in the future because you wear them.

The Lost Art

A gracious woman retains honor.
PROVERBS 11:16 NKJV

The art of graciousness is somewhat lost today. We know how to be cool (what used to be called "hip"), and some even yearn for the unbecoming, seductive title of "hot." But being gracious doesn't seem very popular among today's women. It might be appropriate for the queen of England but definitely not for a young woman who wants to have beauty. Right?

Actually, no. It is a description for any woman, every woman; it is the essence of refined femininity and decorum. We need a return to it.

Beauty in Being Known

For He knows the secrets of the heart.

PSALM 44:21 NKJV

Every woman has secrets.

Events that no one else witnessed.

Feelings that never surface on the outside.

Things known only to her. . .and to God.

We may secretly long for a romance of our own, a child, or a beautiful image. We may be hiding shame over an affair or an abortion. God, the Father, knows. And He wants us to trust Him with our secrets. He wants to show us the beauty of being known and loved and redeemed by His grace.

Cravings Beautified

Delight yourself also in the Lord,
and He will give you the desires
and secret petitions of your heart.
PSALM 37:4 AMPC

What do you crave? Besides chocolate. Or a new pair of shoes.

All of us have longings—things that are often too personal to express.

Our Father in heaven tells us to bring our desires to Him. But first, we are to delight ourselves in Him, find in Him our highest joy. Then our cravings will be framed by our desire for His will in us, and the beauty of that is beyond compare.

Quieted, Beautiful You

I sought the LORD, and He heard me,
and delivered me from all my fears.

PSALM 34:4 NKJV

Your fears make you uniquely you. They reveal what frightens you and show the shape of your personality. In your anxieties, the way your mind works is clearly seen.

Your fears do not put off the Master. He can handle them. He can soothe and calm your spirit. He sees the beauty within and wants to bring it out.

Give your fears to Him. You can be delivered.

He Doesn't Belong

As a ring of gold in a swine's snout,
so is a fair woman who is without discretion.

PROVERBS 11:22 AMPC

If this is true (and the Bible always is), there are many beautiful women in our world today who present an image as awkward as a pig wearing jewelry. The two don't go together.

Today, God wants you to know that you can have beauty and discretion. You can possess beauty and also know how to use it well. You can be good to look at and not be bad for the conscience.

Get rid of the pig. Be beautifully discreet.

Be a Crown

*A virtuous and worthy wife [earnest and
strong in character] is a crowning joy to
her husband, but she who makes him
ashamed is as rottenness in his bones.*
PROVERBS 12:4 AMPC

Wives can be crowns, and they can be cancers. They
can bring shining honor to the men to whom they are
married or eat away at the very core of manhood.

Even if you are unmarried today, you can be a
woman of beautiful character, a woman who possesses
the inner loveliness to crown another with glory.

God wants to use you to shine for Him. Start today.

Beautiful Builders

*The wise woman builds her house,
but the foolish pulls it down with her hands.*

PROVERBS 14:1 NKJV

Many of us know the parable Jesus told about the wise man and the foolish man. We sang the Sunday school song about building on the rock or on the sand. But did you know that there are wise and foolish women, too?

These women either build up or tear down their homes with their own hands. Through attitude, words, choices, and priorities a woman can demonstrate whether she is a builder or a demolitionist.

Which are you?

Past and Present Beauty

*But Mary quietly treasured these things in
her heart and often thought about them.*

LUKE 2:19 TLB

Every memory you have is colored by your perception, your emotion, your vantage point. Your memories, to a large degree, are you. We women treasure memories of special days, events, and emotions.

Today, God wants you to know that you are as beautiful to Him as on that long-ago day when your hair was coiffed and your dress was princesslike. You wish for past beauty, but the reality is that to Him, you are always lovely.

BEAUTIFUL BY EXPERIENCE

Transitions for a Purpose

> To every thing there is a season, and a
> time to every purpose under the heaven.
> ECCLESIASTES 3:1 KJV

"Nothing endures but change" says the old adage. And it does seem true. Nothing lasts forever. Clothes wear out, neighborhoods deteriorate, bodies age, children grow up, spouses die—the earth and people are ever changing. This is the way of life on earth.

Today, God wants you to see that He is using these changing tides to give you more beauty, to shape you after His plan.

Choices about Childhood

When I was a child, I talked like a child,
I thought like a child, I reasoned like a child;
now that I have become a man, I am done
with childish ways and have put them aside.

1 CORINTHIANS 13:11 AMPC

Childhood experiences and events shape the adults we are today. Some had an idyllic childhood; many did not. Whatever your past, God will use it to create beauty in you if you give Him permission to filter it with His grace. Use your maturity to be done with self-pity and make a choice to let the healing begin.

Learning for a Lifetime

"Take My yoke upon you and learn from Me."
MATTHEW 11:29 NKJV

Tiled halls. Metal lockers. Loud bells. One-armed desks. Remember your school days? What did you learn?

Hopefully, you are still benefiting from the days you spent in a classroom. Every one of them is a stroke on the canvas of your life, a contribution to the heart of your being. You're now in God's school of grace. He invites you to get in sync with Him and learn how to do things His way.

It's the way to beautiful living.

Blemishes beyond the Facial Variety

Do not remember the sins of my youth, nor my transgressions; according to Your mercy remember me, for Your goodness' sake, O LORD.

PSALM 25:7 NKJV

Many of the events and decisions we regret occur in our teen years, our adolescence. With the hormonal, emotional, and physical upheaval that is the hallmark of puberty comes a wide-open opportunity for disastrous personal choice.

Maybe that's why the psalmist was anxious to have the Lord forget (redeem and cast away) his youthful indiscretions until only the beauty of those years was seen.

The beauty of a forgiven past can be yours today as well.

Crazy Infatuations

"How beautiful you are, my love, how beautiful!"

SONG OF SOLOMON 4:1 TLB

"I've got a crush on you!"

Not many of us sang those words to the guy we daydreamed about, but there is hardly one of us who hasn't experienced the wild adrenaline rush, flushed cheeks, and erratic heartbeat that accompany an infatuation. Those feelings, in a small way, mirror the heart of a woman, our longings for a great romance.

Today, God wants you to know that He is the longing behind every crush you ever had—and that makes you beautiful to Him.

He Really Sees You

God has said: "I will never
leave you nor forsake you."
HEBREWS 13:5 PHILLIPS

Rejection is hard.

If you've been rejected after tryouts for a sports team, musical auditions, creative writing submissions, college applications, or job interviews, you know the pain.

Personal rejections hurt even more: your mom didn't want you; your boyfriend found someone else; your husband took another woman to his heart; your child wants nothing to do with you. These rejections strike at the heart of our womanhood.

But God sees in you a beauty that the foolish rejections of others cannot diminish.

Whatever Your Résumé

Whatever you do, do well, for in death,
where you are going, there is no working
or planning, or knowing, or understanding.
ECCLESIATES 9:10 TLB

Jobs come and go. We have a variety of them throughout our lifetimes. Some deliver a paycheck; others, like the incredible task of raising kids, do not.

Every job you've ever had becomes part of your beauty when it has passed through the purifying blood of Jesus in that moment of salvation. You can let go of the shame and hold only to the lessons of a life found in Him.

Your résumé: beautified!

Travels

He shall have dominion also from sea to sea,
and from the River to the ends of the earth.

PSALM 72:8 NKJV

Pack your bag and go!

There is exhilaration in seeing new places, eating different foods, and walking unknown paths. Those of us who like to wander a bit may be assured that the magnificence of every exotic place on earth is only a shadow compared to the beauty our God built in the very essence of who we are.

Whether you're sitting on a plane or by your own fireplace, think about that right now.

BEAUTIFUL BY SEASON

Lovely Motherhood

*He shall feed his flock like a shepherd:
he shall gather the lambs with his arm,
and carry them in his bosom, and shall
gently lead those that are with young.*

ISAIAH 40:11 KJV

God believes in motherhood. He created women, invented the process of procreation and birth, and sent His own Son to a womb on earth.

God affirms the emotions of motherhood; He delights in the beauty of motherhood. And He gently leads those who are tending young.

Today, He wants you to know that motherhood looks great on you.

Age Doesn't Matter

*Charm and grace are deceptive, and beauty
is vain [because it is not lasting], but a woman
who reverently and worshipfully fears the
Lord, she shall be praised!*
PROVERBS 31:30 AMPC

Aging is not supposed to be beautiful. It is, after all, a fading of our vibrancy and tautness, a decline into less color and more sags. No woman longs for that.

God's Word tells us that earthly physical beauty isn't lasting. We must cement our identity, not in how we look, but in who He is in us.

And His eyes see your essence anyway, regardless of the skin.

The Day of You

A good name is better than precious
perfume, and the day of death better
than the day of one's birth.

ECCLESIASTES 7:1 AMPC

Birthdays remind us that life is a moving line, a continuum. We aren't standing still here. Birthdays tell us that we have passed through another yearly cycle of seasons—spring, summer, fall, and winter. Birthdays are a one-day celebration that is determined by the other 364. Birthdays remind us that living takes a while to do.

And each day crossed off the calendar makes us just a little more beautiful in God.

Endless Process

*Being confident of this very thing, that He
who has begun a good work in you will
complete it until the day of Jesus Christ.*

PHILIPPIANS 1:6 NKJV

The growing process includes awkward stages, whether in plants, animals, or humans. Fragile green sprouts hardly have the lush contours of ripe vegetables; spindly pupa and tiny tadpoles do not look like their adult destiny, and the oversize heads and pudgy legs of human toddlers are cute but not streamlined.

Womanhood, like other growth, is a process. God began it in you when you were conceived and continues it to this very day.

Every Single Day

"As long as the earth remains, there will be springtime and harvest, cold and heat, winter and summer, day and night."

GENESIS 8:22 TLB

Do you have a favorite season?

Today, whatever season of the year it is outside, you are on God's mind. In the spring, He likes you in pastels. In the summer, He delights in your joy of going barefoot. In the fall, He looks at you with love in your sweater and scarf. And in the winter, He smiles at the snowflakes in your hair.

Every single day of the year you are His beloved.

Holidays

A feast is made for laughter.

ECCLESIASTES 10:19 NKJV

If you like holidays, you're not alone. Most of us enjoy something about them, whether it's just the break from work or the actual family time and food or the significance of the day itself. Holidays just seem a bit more joyful than the average day. But as far as you're concerned, God puts no more emphasis on a holiday than on a Monday. He celebrates the wonder of you every day.

Rainy Days

"He gives rain on the earth,
and sends waters on the fields."

JOB 5:10 NKJV

Karen Carpenter crooned, "Rainy days and Mondays always get me down."

Maybe you feel like that. Perhaps the gray skies and sloshy puddles make you feel sad. Or maybe you relish a good rainy day now and then, enjoying a bowl of soup and a favorite book. God knows which is your tendency. And He wants to be part of every rainy day you have. Trust Him when the clouds start to roll in. He is still watching out for you.

BEAUTIFUL THROUGH REDEMPTION

Holy Beauty

*So that he could give her to himself
as a glorious Church without a single
spot or wrinkle or any other blemish,
being holy and without a single fault.*

EPHESIANS 5:27 TLB

Christ died to make the Church, His bride, holy. He did for her what she could not do herself.

If you have given your heart to Him, you are more than part of the collective bride of Christ; you are an individual, beloved by Him, beautified through His sacrifice on the cross.

No price was too high for Him to ensure your holy beauty.

Through and Through

*For the word of God is living and powerful,
and sharper than any two-edged sword, piercing
even to the division of soul and spirit, and of
joints and marrow, and is a discerner of the
thoughts and intents of the heart.*

<small>HEBREWS 4:12 NKJV</small>

Have you ever been around a woman who was beautiful to you until you saw her motives? Someone with gorgeous features can be driven by hideous, selfish, conniving desires.

God wants us to be lovely through and through. He has given us His Word to show us where we need His power to make us that way.

Made to Hold His Glory

Being filled with the fruits of righteousness,
which are by Jesus Christ, unto the
glory and praise of God.

PHILIPPIANS 1:11 KJV

God does not want you to be an empty beauty.

He takes no delight in a beautiful but barren container. You were made to hold His righteousness and His glory. Sin defiled us and made us unfit for Him. But through the redemption offered in Christ, it is now possible for us to have His very life within us. That is the ultimate beauty treatment. He holds it out to you.

Kept like a Princess

*You, who are kept by the power
of God through faith for salvation.*

1 PETER 1:4–5 NKJV

A trend in decorating refers to the main room in a house as the "keeping room." The term dates back to Colonial times, referring to a large multiuse room attached to the kitchen area.

God has you in a "keeping room." If you belong to Him, you are surrounded by His power and covered from anything outside of His will for you. He has you in the palm of His hand. Like a princess protected by a knight, you are safe.

He Holds the Mirror

And such were some of you. But you were washed, but you were sanctified, but you were justified, in the name of the Lord Jesus and by the Spirit of our God.

1 Corinthians 6:11 NKJV

Those who belong to Christ have been changed.

Maybe in the past you have had unhealthy views of your identity and your need to attract the eyes and desires of men. But when Christ holds the mirror for us, we can look in it and see the truth that we are changed. His love and approval are now the standard for our beauty.

Beautiful like Zion

*Out of Zion, the perfection
of beauty, God hath shined.*
PSALM 50:2 KJV

*I have likened the daughter of Zion
to a comely and delicate woman.*
JEREMIAH 6:2 KJV

Zion is the symbol of God's presence, His dwelling place. The "daughter of Zion" is a biblical name for Jerusalem, the Holy City.

God chose to characterize these hallowed places using the idea of beauty. Our God created and blesses the concept of holy beauty. You were created to reflect it.

Today, choose to let His holiness illuminate your life and make you beautiful.

Justified and Peaceful

Therefore being justified by faith, we have peace with God through our Lord Jesus Christ.

ROMANS 5:1 KJV

In itself, beauty does not bring peace. It is a source of stress and envy, of endless searching. There is always a new diet to try or fitness program to embrace. There is no end to the choices in cosmetics, hair color and skin products, enhancement surgeries and facelifts. The carousel never stops.

We must approach our God-given beauty with the knowledge that it is being justified by faith that gives us peace. And the carousel ride doesn't make us dizzy anymore.

Set-Apart Beauty

*Therefore if anyone cleanses himself from
the latter, he will be a vessel for honor,
sanctified and useful for the Master,
prepared for every good work.*

2 TIMOTHY 2:21 NKJV

To be sanctified is to be set apart, made ready for a sacred purpose. God wants not only to justify us, forgive our sins, but also to sanctify us, to make us holy and ready for His use.

Much of the beauty in our world today is self-absorbed and self-gratifying. We are to be different.

Today, surrender your beauty to Him and discover the joy of being set apart, sanctified.

BEAUTIFUL THROUGH GRACE

Holy Adrenaline

*As you live this new life, we pray that you will be
strengthened from God's boundless resources,
so that you will find yourselves able to pass through
any experience and endure it with courage.*

COLOSSIANS 1:11 PHILLIPS

God living inside us through His Holy Spirit gives us
power, a kind of holy adrenaline. You may be a single woman. You may have lost a spouse. You may be
surrounded by children and their needs. You may be in a
difficult marriage. Whatever the place, God has promised
you the resources through His grace to live there.

Support When Needed

*Cast your burden on the LORD,
and He shall sustain you.*

PSALM 55:22 NKJV

Sometimes we women just need a little support!

Life has many details to manage and people to nurture. As the God-gifted multitaskers in the family, women are pretty good at juggling schedules and meals and errands and appointments. But we also have burdens. And it is hard to revel in the beauty of life if we're bogged down with stuff. So the Father tells us to let Him help us carry the load.

Today, He wants you to know that you are not alone.

Not a Fragile Sentiment

"I am leaving you with a gift—peace of mind and heart! And the peace I give isn't fragile like the peace the world gives. So don't be troubled or afraid."

JOHN 14:27 TLB

Womanhood is an assignment.

You are called to live on this earth as a female bearer of God's image, to interact with others and glorify Him through that template. He has given you personal beauty and a womanly perspective as well as the wondrous treasure of His peace—not a fragile, wispy sentiment but a stable, supportive assurance that will go with you and keep you.

Beautifully Open

*"A good man out of the good treasure of his heart
brings forth good; and an evil man out of the evil
treasure of his heart brings forth evil. For out of the
abundance of the heart his mouth speaks."*

LUKE 6:45 NKJV

God's grace at work gives us the strength to be
vulnerable and open, to share the "treasure" within,
our inner beauty, thoughts, dreams, and longings. Satan
wants to wall up our beauty, to make us closed and
fearful, bitter and cynical. But Christ conquered him and
gives us the grace to be beautifully open, reflecting Him.

Say No to Pouting

*Never act from motives of rivalry or
personal vanity, but in humility think more
of each other than you do of yourselves.*
PHILIPPIANS 2:3 PHILLIPS

You know the story of the pampered, pouty princess, right?

Well, maybe Disney never made a movie about her, but there is certainly the temptation to take on that persona. Beauty that is turned inward sours. It turns to ugliness.

Today, God wants you to know that your beauty is meant to be selfless. He gave His grace to you; you are to share it with others.

Best Beauty Secret

Yes, all of you be submissive to one another,
and be clothed with humility, for "God resists
the proud, but gives grace to the humble."
1 PETER 5:5 NKJV

"If you've got it, flaunt it."

That's the philosophy of the culture around us. We are encouraged to use our beauty for our own means, to draw attention to ourselves for our own indulgence.

God says for us to be clothed, not with our own pride, but with humility. This attitude comes from His grace within, the best beauty secret around.

Focused on Gratefulness

Be thankful unto him, and bless his name.
PSALM 100:4 KJV

One of the most beautiful spirits is gratefulness.

It is sometimes difficult to exhibit gratefulness when you're unhappy with your features or your wardrobe or your shoe size or a multitude of other aspects about appearance.

But being thankful for the traits you do enjoy will make today even more beautiful. As the old song says "Accentuate the positive." For a Christian woman, that means focus on the good features God has given you.

Accepting His Time

Therefore submit to God.

JAMES 4:7 NKJV

Amy Carmichael, a woman who fought sex trafficking many years ago in the country of India, said, "In acceptance lieth peace."

She certainly had much opportunity to test this theory. A single woman in a foreign land, head of a large ministry, and struggling with chronic illness in her later years, Amy proved the value of surrender in her life. She left her wisdom to us in poems and prose.

What do you need to submit to God today? Accept His will; trust Him to make your life beautiful in His time.

Empowered to Love

All the special gifts and powers from
God will someday come to an end,
but love goes on forever.

1 Corinthians 13:8 tlb

Love is perhaps the Christian virtue most discussed today, but it is not primarily an emotion; it is an action.

Love stems from a choice to seek the good of another, to be kind, to show mercy, and to give expecting nothing in return.

We as women who know Christ are to exemplify love in our daily lives. We can do this practically by affirming others. Give a compliment to someone today. That's beautifully loving.

BEAUTIFUL THROUGH PRAYER

Better Than the Spa

Blessed are those who keep His testimonies,
who seek Him with the whole heart!
PSALM 119:2 NKJV

Today, God wants you to see Him with your whole heart. He wants you to know that being in relationship with Him is the one way to fully realize your personal beauty. You may seek after many things, but only an ongoing pursuit of Him, His person, and His leading in your life will truly make you a more complete person.

Talking to Him every day is the way to seek Him. Prayer is better than the spa.

His Whispers to You

Let my prayer come before You;
incline Your ear to my cry.

PSALM 88:2 NKJV

God knows you like no other. He delights in you as a unique person, endowed with His image and made for a specific, glorious purpose. You are not a random combination of skin and bones and blood. You are a masterpiece. Your complexity points to the magnificence of the Almighty. You will know this more fully as you take time to communicate with Him every day.

Today, He wants to whisper in your ear how very special you are.

Prayer as a Beauty Routine

You will show me the path of life;
in Your presence is fullness of joy.

PSALM 16:11 NKJV

The best time of the day is your beauty routine. Not putting on your cosmetics, but spending time in God's presence. Talking to the Lord brings perspective like nothing else. Being in His presence gives joy, which always beautifies.

Want big, beautiful eyes? Ask Him to widen them with pure delight in His world today.

Tired of wrinkles? Worry less; trust more.

Reflect His glory everywhere you go.

This is the way He beautifies His beloved.

Prayer Equals Radiance

Moses didn't realize as he came back down the mountain with the tablets that his face glowed from being in the presence of God.

EXODUS 34:29 TLB

Every woman wants her face to have that radiant, healthy glow. No cosmetic can deliver like time spent with God.

Moses had to wear a veil because his face was so bright. Yours probably won't be like that, but if you create space in your day to talk to God, you will have a radiance that others will notice.

The Right Mirror

But the man who looks into the perfect mirror
of God's law, the law of liberty (or freedom),
and makes a habit of so doing, is not the man
who sees and forgets. He puts that law into
practice and he wins true happiness.

JAMES 1:25 PHILLIPS

Women have a love-hate relationship with mirrors.

The most important mirror is God's Word. It shows
us who we really are and what we need to do to enhance
our soul beauty. God wants you to exchange your mirror
for His; it tells the truth.

BEAUTIFUL IN PAIN

Suffering to Be Beautiful

*Now obviously no "chastening" seems
pleasant at the time: it is in fact most
unpleasant. Yet when it is all over we can
see that [it] has quietly produced the fruit
of real goodness in the characters of those
who have accepted it in the right spirit.*

HEBREWS 12:11 PHILLIPS

"You have to suffer to be beautiful."

My mom used to say these words to me when I, as a child, was protesting her efforts to fix my hair. The beauty routine God creates for us also involves some pain. But it has great reward. Let it work for you.

Priority Despite Pain

*And behold, there was a woman who had a spirit
of infirmity eighteen years, and was bent over
and could in no way raise herself up. But when
Jesus saw her, He called her to Him and said to
her, "Woman, you are loosed from your infirmity."
And He laid His hands on her, and immediately
she was made straight, and glorified God.*

LUKE 13:11–13 NKJV

It sure sounds like osteoporosis. But this woman, though she hadn't walked straight for eighteen years, was still coming to worship, was still giving God priority in her life.

Give Him priority despite your pain.

Birthing Is Beautiful

*"When a woman gives birth to a child,
she certainly knows pain when her time comes.
Yet as soon as she has given birth to the child,
she no longer remembers her agony for joy that
a man has been born into the world."*

JOHN 16:21 PHILLIPS

Birth is beautiful, though women are really working hard in the process. Birthing a child is a sweaty, bloody, messy business. Not to mention painful.

But when the baby is born, glistening and squalling, the mother begins to forget the terror and trauma of labor. She has given life to a child. And it is beautiful.

You can do hard things beautifully.

Barren to Beautiful

He gives children to the childless wife,
so that she becomes a happy mother.
Hallelujah! Praise the Lord.
PSALM 113:9 TLB

Barrenness in biblical days was a life sentence of humiliation and possibly poverty. A childless woman was pitied, and people often wondered if she was being judged by God for some secret sin.

So when a woman in the Bible rejoiced over the birth of a child, she was actually expressing deep gratitude for God's provision on so many levels. This psalm declares that God is so mighty that He can cause even a barren woman to give birth. What a beautiful statement of power!

For Women Only

And behold, a woman who had suffered from a flow of blood for twelve years came up behind Him and touched the fringe of His garment; for she kept saying to herself, If I only touch His garment, I shall be restored to health. Jesus turned around and, seeing her, He said, Take courage, daughter! Your faith has made you well. And at once the woman was restored to health.

MATTHEW 9:20–22 AMPC

In that culture and because of the social mores related to purification under the Mosaic law, a woman with a menstrual disorder was socially unacceptable. Anyone who touched her was unclean. Yet this woman risked reaching out to Jesus. And He healed her.

Not Forsaken

Then they all forsook Him and fled.

MARK 14:50 NKJV

Are you lonely?

Jesus was, too. His best friends ran away from Him on the worst night of His life. Maybe you've been there. The pain of loneliness is one most of us have felt.

A perk of being one of the "beautiful" people is that admirers flock to you; crowds want to be close to someone who has it all. But God wants you to know that your level of popularity isn't a factor with Him. And the beauty of your smile always draws Him to you.

Don't Compare; Be Content

But they, measuring themselves by
themselves, and comparing themselves
among themselves, are not wise.

2 Corinthians 10:12 NKJV

How clever of Satan to get us to think that beauty pageants are fun and glamorous when really they make us run amok in envy and resentment and depression. At the very least, they encourage us to focus on outward beauty to the exclusion of inward loveliness.

It is unwise to compare your beauty with another woman God made. He did His best work on you, as He did on her. So be content to celebrate your own unique place in His heart.

Longing for Health

Have mercy upon me, O LORD;
for I am weak: O LORD, heal me.

PSALM 6:2 KJV

Our culture reveres health and fitness. Trends of eating organic, taking whole food supplements, and using essential oils and herbs bear testament to our fascination with natural health.

But our society is also plagued with diseases of the body and mind. Your beauty does not rely on you being 100 percent healthy. Your beauty is not only of the body but mostly of the soul. No pain you feel can make it disappear.

Conditioned through Misunderstanding

"My best friends abhor me.
Those I loved have turned against me."

JOB 19:19 TLB

Yeah, girlfriend, sometimes we are misunderstood. Big-time. And people rarely give us credit for our intentions.

It's hard to feel beautiful when you are rejected. Today, if that is you, know that God is aware of the whole story and wants to be your strength as you figure out how to get things back on track. The pain of being misunderstood can actually work beauty in you; let Him show you how.

Reasons for Praise

But, O my soul, don't be discouraged. Don't be upset. Expect God to act! For I know that I shall again have plenty of reason to praise him for all that he will do. He is my help! He is my God!

PSALM 42:11 TLB

Being beautiful is no immunity from depression. In fact, beauty without godliness just might put you at greater danger for this emotional illness.

But if you know Christ as your Savior, your beauty is safeguarded by His peace. You can expect God to act in your life, and you have plenty of reason to praise Him.

Not the Permanent Image

He has not dealt with us according to our sins,
nor punished us according to our iniquities.
For as the heavens are high above the earth,
so great is His mercy toward those who fear Him.
PSALM 103:10–11 NKJV

You are beautiful in your failure.

Yes, you are. God's image in you is not erased because of your sin, though it is damaged, marred. But that doesn't have to be the permanent, defining statement about you. Let Him restore to fullness the beauty that He still sees in you.

Beauty for Brokenness

*"The Lord your God in your midst, the Mighty One,
will save; He will rejoice over you with gladness,
He will quiet you with His love, He will
rejoice over you with singing."*

ZEPHANIAH 3:17 NKJV

You are beautiful to God just because He made you. He invented you. He thought up the idea of you.

But you can choose to embrace even more beauty by responding to His call of salvation. When you let Him redeem the broken places in you, you will reflect His beauty even more fully. He will quiet you and rejoice over you.

BEAUTIFUL IN TRIUMPH

Blessed by Providence

*"So you shall rejoice in every good thing
which the LORD your God has given to you."*
DEUTERONOMY 26:11 NKJV

You are beautiful when you give praise to God for His blessings on you.

As Christian women, we don't put stock in random. We affirm providence, His providence. Sometimes He gives trials, but when He sends blessings, we joyfully accept and celebrate.

Let His beauty be seen in you by the way you acknowledge Him in your good things.

Victorious Warrior Princess

*Blessed be the LORD my Rock, who trains
my fingers for battle.*

PSALM 144:1 NKJV

You are beautiful in battle—a battle against the Enemy,
Satan.

No doubt the warrior-king David was speaking here about actual physical battle; he waged a lot
of them. But we can be just as sure that our heavenly
King will prepare us to fight the wiles of the devil. No
fiery dart has to take us down. He has trained us well.

You are more beautiful, more victorious than Joan
of Arc. You are God's warrior-princess. Today, you stand.

An Almost Perfect Day

Let the heavens rejoice, and let the earth be glad;
let the sea roar, and the fulness thereof.

PSALM 96:11 KJV

Once in a while, it happens. You wake up feeling refreshed and your coffee is just right and your outfit looks so good and you make it to work with little traffic, or the children get up without a fuss and you remember to take the meat out of the freezer and you even find a five-dollar bill in your pocket. A really good day.

Celebrate this lovely day from God. And let the world sing with you.

The Good News

This was the LORD's doing;
it is marvelous in our eyes.
PSALM 118:23 NKJV

The test was negative! God answered your prayer.

If you've ever waited on the results of a medical test, you know the anxiety that creeps over you. It seems the whole world is at a standstill, everything in your life is on tiptoe, holding its breath.

It is a beautiful thing to absorb God's mercy in allowing you to escape a disease or terminal diagnosis. Let it seep into your heart and transform your outlook.

BEAUTIFUL IN SACRIFICE

Keeping Silent

Set a watch, O LORD, before my mouth;
keep the door of my lips.
PSALM 141:3 KJV

You are beautiful when you are silent. And you are beautiful when you speak. Knowing when to speak and when not to speak is so important.

Ecclesiastes 3 says there is a time for silence. If it is your time to do that, then being silent beautifies you the most right now. The Holy Spirit who lives within nudges us when we should not speak. Never ignore it.

Restraint of any kind is a sacrifice of action. But it usually makes you more beautiful.

Bearing Insult

A man does something valuable when
he endures pain, as in the sight of God,
though he knows he is suffering unjustly.

1 PETER 2:19 PHILLIPS

We are taught to value justice in America. And speaking up for ourselves. And personal boundaries to protect ourselves from exploitation.

God does want us to use good relational skills. But there are times when the most godly and the most beautiful thing you can do is bear an insult with a sweet spirit, not trying to correct it but letting it go.

God keeps excellent records. All will be turned right someday.

Beautifully Doing Without

But I discipline my body and bring it into subjection, lest, when I have preached to others, I myself should become disqualified.

1 CORINTHIANS 9:27 NKJV

Most of us have more than enough. You can show uncommon beauty by doing without. You can give to someone else. You can deprive yourself of some indulgence just for the sake of the discipline of restraint.

More than giving up something like sweets for a few weeks, you can practice a life of structuring those desires that tend to run rampant if left to themselves. And in doing so, you will gain even more beauty.

Time for Others

*And I will very gladly spend
and be spent for your souls.*

2 CORINTHIANS 12:15 NKJV

It is a beautiful thing to give your resources for another.

Time is a precious resource for us all. Choosing to focus on the needs of someone else is a lovely gift. The apostle Paul was speaking in a spiritual sense in this verse, but the principle says that love is willing to expend itself.

To whom, for whom, are you willing to give your time?

BEAUTIFUL IN SURRENDER

Surrendered Beauty Routine

For you were bought at a price;
therefore glorify God in your body
and in your spirit, which are God's.

1 CORINTHIANS 6:20 NKJV

Surrender your beauty routine to God.

Yes, He cares about that. What you wear. How you style your hair. How you adorn your body. He cares because, if you have trusted Him for salvation, you belong to Him, and your body is His temple. It is also a witness to others about who is in charge of your life.

So ask Him how He wants you to look.

Practice the beautiful grace of surrender.

Dream His Dreams

*I realise that everyone has his own particular gift
from God, some one thing and some another.*

1 Corinthians 7:7 phillips

Most of us don't agree with the apostle that celibacy is a good thing. We long for romance, a meaningful relationship on which to build a marriage and family. But Paul said that some are gifted with singleness.

Christians are called to surrender, to acknowledge God's lordship over every area of our lives, even and especially this one.

Surrender your dreams of romance to the One who loves you most, and trust Him to give you a beautiful life in return.

How to Hold On to Family

My lord, O king, according to thy saying,
I am thine, and all that I have.

1 KINGS 20:4 KJV

We must hold God's gifts with open hands. We cannot clutch to ourselves anything that issues from His goodness.

Family is the most basic and the most precious of gifts. Like the man in this biblical story from Israel's history, we need to come before our King and tell Him that all we have, including the family He has given, belongs to Him.

Directed Life

*A man's heart plans his way,
but the LORD directs his steps.*

PROVERBS 16:9 NKJV

You have plans for your life. That's good. God put within us a desire to act and accomplish. But this must never take precedence over God's will for us.

The key to a beautiful life is not an expensive education or cosmopolitan travel or an affluent lifestyle with a successful career. No, the key to living beautifully is surrendering your ideas to the light of His will. He will show you the path of life.

He Owns Your Day

The day is Yours, the night also is Yours;
You have prepared the light and the sun.

PSALM 74:16 NKJV

God owns the day and the night.

He owns this day. Whatever it is in the week, wherever it is on the calendar. With all its humdrum, catastrophe, or surprises, He owns it.

By your own will, give today to Him. Let Him own it a second time, because you surrender it to Him. The beauty of a day that belongs to Him will amaze you.

Surrendered Gifts

*Every good gift and every perfect gift is
from above, and comes down from the
Father of lights, with whom there is no
variation or shadow of turning.*

JAMES 1:17 NKJV

Anything you have or enjoy that is positive and pleasant is from God. He is the only one with the capability
and the nature to give these blessings. We humans
cannot give them to ourselves. And Satan will never
give us anything truly good, only things that look good
to bait us.

Because we know the Giver, we can surrender our
blessings back to Him.

Future Times Are His

And He said to them, "It is not for you to know times or seasons which the Father has put in His own authority."

ACTS 1:7 NKJV

Surrender your future to God.

He has not given us all the information about what is coming in world events. He does not even tell us what we can expect in our own individual lives, except to promise us that He will be with us every minute.

Living an anxious, fearful life is not His will. Living in trusting, surrendered relationship with Him is what He intended for you all along.

Wardrobe Issues

In like manner also, that the women
adorn themselves in modest apparel,
with propriety and moderation.

1 TIMOTHY 2:9 NKJV

God cares about what you wear.

The only way you can glorify God to others is through what they can see in you. Let the advertisement that you are be one that brings Him honor. Be appropriate and moderate and modest. This is true beauty. Excess of either adornment or exposed skin contradicts the goal of letting Him be the beauty shining through. Don't let your earthly beauty obscure His holy beauty.

BEAUTIFUL IN WORSHIP

Made Beautiful through Worship

*I will praise him as long as I live, yes,
even with my dying breath.*
PSALM 146:2 TLB

A woman who worships God is beautiful. Bringing praise to the One who made her and gifted her makes her more lovely.

Culture tells us that beautiful women are to be worshipped.

God's Word tells us that women are to give worship and thus be beautiful.

Who will you believe today?

Worshipful Hearts

I will praise You with my whole heart;
before the gods I will sing praises to You.

PSALM 138:1 NKJV

Lift your heart to the One who has redeemed you, to the One who keeps you and watches over you.

Today, He really cares about you. He knows what is going on in your life. Praise Him with your whole heart. Sing praises to Him.

When the heart is praising, the countenance is glistening.

BEAUTIFUL IN GROWTH

Beautiful Blooming

Those who are planted in the house of the
LORD shall flourish in the courts of our God.

PSALM 92:13 NKJV

Growth is a beautiful thing.

Whether a poppy in the field, a tree in the forest, or a vegetable in the garden, things that bud and blossom and bloom are wondrous sights to behold. God's Word says that those who put their roots down in the soil of God's kingdom will flourish. They will not wither but grow and give beauty to all around.

It's a Process

*But grow in grace, and in the knowledge
of our Lord and Saviour Jesus Christ.*

2 PETER 3:18 KJV

The only thing that grows overnight is the beanstalk in the fairy tale about the giant. In real life, growing things involves a process.

It's the same with your journey in godly womanhood. You must stay in the sunshine of God's love and refuse to wilt in the rain. If you stay connected to Him, the source of life, you will grow into mature beauty.

Growth in Trust

"Consider how the wild flowers grow. They neither work nor weave, but I tell you that even Solomon in all his glory was never arrayed like one of these! Now if God so clothes the flowers of the field, which are alive today and burnt in the stove tomorrow, is he not much more likely to clothe you, you 'little-faiths'?"

MATTHEW 6:28–30 PHILLIPS

Just like a beautiful flower in the field which does nothing to earn the sunshine and rain and which doesn't create its own lovely petals, you are to look up and trust God for what you need.

Use Your Will

*And beside this, giving all diligence, add to
your faith virtue; and to virtue knowledge.*

2 PETER 1:5 KJV

God wants you to grow in understanding. And you have
a part to play in it. We are different from the flowers
of the field in that we have a say in our growth. While
only God can produce growth in us through His holy
power, we can say yes or no to His efforts.

Use your will to affirm that you will do everything you can to cooperate with His process of growth
in you.

Witness to Growth

"But you are to be given power when the Holy Spirit has come to you. You will be witnesses to me, not only in Jerusalem, not only throughout Judea, not only in Samaria, but to the very ends of the earth!"

ACTS 1:8 PHILLIPS

God's power at work in you is calling you to witness for Him, both in your words and in your manner of living. This is an area in which He wants you to grow. When you shine for Him, you are beautiful, for everything and every person He indwells has the beauty of His holiness within.

Love More

*"This is My commandment, that you
love one another as I have loved you."*

JOHN 15:12 NKJV

Keeping God's commandments brings out His beauty in you. Commandments were not made to stifle beauty but to frame it and protect it, to make it the way it was meant to be.

A woman who reflects His divine love to those around her is a beautiful woman. Her actions and attitudes are layered in His gentle strength.

Today, God wants to help you grow in your love for others.

BEAUTIFUL AND BIBLICAL

Anna: Beauty of Praise

Now there was one, Anna, a prophetess, the daughter of Phanuel, of the tribe of Asher. She was of a great age, and had lived with a husband seven years from her virginity; and this woman was a widow of about eighty-four years, who did not depart from the temple, but served God with fastings and prayers night and day. And coming in that instant she gave thanks to the Lord, and spoke of Him to all those who looked for redemption in Jerusalem.

LUKE 2:36–38 NKJV

Anna literally lived to praise God. She was one of the first human beings and probably the first woman besides Mary to recognize Jesus as the Messiah. When He was brought to the temple as an infant, she was there to glorify Him. That's how to be beautiful even at age eighty-four!

Esther: Beauty Prepared

*And Mordecai had brought up Hadassah, that is,
Esther, his uncle's daughter, for she had neither
father nor mother. The young woman was lovely and
beautiful. . . . The king loved Esther more than all the
other women, and she obtained grace and favor in his
sight more than all the virgins; so he set the royal crown
upon her head and made her queen instead of Vashti.*

ESTHER 2:7, 17 NKJV

God had prepared Esther for the work she needed to
do—being a queen to a pagan king. He has prepared
you also for something. Discover what it is and do it
for His glory.

Ruth: Beauty of Soul

And Boaz answered and said to her, "It has been fully reported to me, all that you have done for your mother-in-law since the death of your husband, and how you have left your father and your mother and the land of your birth, and have come to a people whom you did not know before."

RUTH 2:11 NKJV

Ruth gave herself for others. She was willing to sacrifice. As a foreigner in a strange land, she pushed down her fears and served. Perhaps she was beautiful in face and form as well, but her personal beauty of soul was greater.

Abigail: Beauty and Wisdom

*His name was Nabal and his wife, a beautiful
and very intelligent woman, was named Abigail.
But the man, who was a descendant of Caleb, was
uncouth, churlish, stubborn, and ill-mannered. . . .
David replied to Abigail, "Bless the Lord God of
Israel who has sent you to meet me today!
Thank God for your good sense! Bless you for
keeping me from murdering the man and carrying
out vengeance with my own hands."*

1 SAMUEL 25:3, 32–33 TLB

Abigail was not only beautiful; she was wise. God used
her to avert a tragedy. God wants you to be wise today.

Sarah: Beauty of Spirit

*And when he was about to enter into
Egypt, he said to Sarai his wife, I know
that you are beautiful to behold.*

GENESIS 12:11 AMPC

*For in this manner, in former times, the holy women
who trusted in God also adorned themselves, being
submissive to their own husbands, as Sarah obeyed
Abraham, calling him lord, whose daughters you are
if you do good and are not afraid with any terror.*

1 PETER 3:5–6 NKJV

Sarah was physically beautiful, even in old age. But
the Bible commends her more for her beautiful spirit.
Follow her example to be truly beautiful.

Hannah:
Beauty of Surrender

*And she made this vow: "O Lord of heaven, if you
will look down upon my sorrow and answer my
prayer and give me a son, then I will give him back
to you, and he'll be yours for his entire lifetime,
and his hair shall never be cut."*

1 SAMUEL 1:11 TLB

Hannah surrendered her longing to the God of heaven.
She asked for a son—a male child to fill her heart and
remove the humiliation of infertility, which was so great
in her culture. She promised her son to God to be
consecrated as a Nazarite, and she kept her promise.

Rachel and Leah: Beauty That Divided

Leah's eyes were delicate, but Rachel was beautiful of form and appearance.

GENESIS 29:17 NKJV

Two sisters. The same man. Sounds like a twenty-first-century soap opera.

This one was real. And the twists and turns are heart wrenching. Jacob loved Rachel more, but we see later in the story that hers was a conniving beauty.

Don't let personal beauty and the men it attracts divide you from your sisters in Christ.

Rebekah: Beauty of Working

As he was still speaking to the Lord about this, a beautiful young girl named Rebekah arrived with a water jug on her shoulder and filled it at the spring. . . . So they called Rebekah. "Are you willing to go with this man?" they asked her. And she replied, "Yes, I will go."

GENESIS 24:15, 58 TLB

Abraham's servant was looking for a wife for Isaac. God led him to Rebekah. She was working, doing her daily tasks.

Today, God wants to use your faithful attention to life's little details to bless someone else. It's a beauty often overlooked.

Eve: Womanly Design

Then the rib which the LORD God had taken from man He made into a woman, and He brought her to the man. . . . And Adam called his wife's name Eve, because she was the mother of all living.

GENESIS 2:22; 3:20 NKJV

Eve was the first one, the very first woman God crafted. In her, He expressed His grand plan for womanhood—no doubt beautiful, graceful, delicate of form yet strong of heart, perfectly suited to be a companion, a partner for Adam.

You bear a remnant of her glory. Use it today to honor Him.

Mary, Mother of Jesus: Beautiful in Sacrifice

The virgin's name was Mary. . . . Then Mary said,
"Behold the maidservant of the Lord! Let it
be to me according to your word."
LUKE 1:27, 38 NKJV

And Mary said: "My soul magnifies the Lord,
and my spirit has rejoiced in God my Savior."
LUKE 1:46–47 NKJV

Mary, the mother of Jesus, sacrificed her plans, dreams, and reputation to allow God's will in her life. While we don't know about her outward beauty, we can witness the loveliness of her submission to His plan.

Today, determine to place yourself second to His will for you.

Dorcas: Beauty of Nature

*At Joppa there was a certain disciple named
Tabitha, which is translated Dorcas. This woman
was full of good works and charitable deeds. . . .
And all the widows stood by [Peter] weeping,
showing the tunics and garments which Dorcas
had made while she was with them.*

ACTS 9:36, 39 NKJV

Dorcas was a woman who used her natural gifts to bless
others. She knew how to sew. What do you know how
to do? What has God put into your nature that you can
use as a means of beautiful service?

Rhoda: Beauty of Service

As he knocked at the door a young maid called Rhoda came to answer it.

ACTS 12:13 PHILLIPS

Servanthood in Jesus' day was common. Many people were subjugated by another nation or had to sell themselves as servants to pay off debts. The economic classes of the time were distinctly separated.

Rhoda was a servant. We don't know much about her, but she was serving while the church was praying. She was filling her assigned role.

Maybe you are in a lowly place today. Make it beautiful by opening doors for others.

Lois and Eunice: Beauty of Faithfulness

*I often think of that genuine faith of yours—
a faith that first appeared in your grandmother
Lois, then in Eunice your mother, and is now,
I am convinced, in you as well.*

2 TIMOTHY 1:5 PHILLIPS

The young preacher Timothy had an advantage. He had been nurtured by two godly women: his grandmother Lois and his mother, Eunice. This mother and daughter, or mother-in-law and daughter-in-law, raised a young man who would bless many.

How does God want you to nurture someone today? Do it; it will beautify you as well.

Mary Magdalene: Beauty of Worship

Now when He rose early on the first day of the week, He appeared first to Mary Magdalene, out of whom He had cast seven demons.

MARK 16:9 NKJV

Mary of Magdala was probably a well-known sinner in her town. She was possessed by seven demons. She no doubt had a reputation.

When Jesus redeemed her and gave her back her life, she loved Him and followed Him ever after, even helping to bury Him and mourning at His tomb on the resurrection morning.

Her heart was beautiful in worship.

Joanna: Serving Him

Joanna the wife of Chuza, Herod's steward, and Susanna, and many others who provided for Him from their substance.

LUKE 8:3 NKJV

It was Mary Magdalene, Joanna, Mary the mother of James, and the other women with them, who told these things to the apostles.

LUKE 24:10 NKJV

Joanna is one of the women you don't hear much about. But she was a faithful follower of Christ, giving of her own resources to fund His ministry and His well-being, and one of the women who went to the tomb early to wrap His body with spices.

Her beauty was in "doing" for Him.

Miriam: Beautiful in Triumph

*Then Miriam the prophetess, the sister of Aaron,
took a tambourine and led the women in dances.
And Miriam sang this song: Sing to the Lord,
for he has triumphed gloriously. The horse
and rider have been drowned in the sea.*

EXODUS 15:20–21 TLB

The nation of Israel was free! Miriam led the women in a song of triumph. There on the shores of the Red Sea, she praised God for all to see.

Today, God wants to be glorified in your beautiful song of triumph.

Deborah: Beautiful in Her Season

*Now Deborah, a prophetess, the wife of Lapidoth,
was judging Israel at that time. And she would sit
under the palm tree of Deborah between Ramah
and Bethel in the mountains of Ephraim. And the
children of Israel came up to her for judgment.*

JUDGES 4:4–5 NKJV

Not many women in Israel held the title of prophetess.
But, however out of the ordinary it was, Deborah
accepted this role and filled her place in this season
of the judges.

In what unusual place does God want you to be
beautiful right now?

Shulamite: Beautiful in Celebration

*O my love, you are as beautiful as Tirzah, lovely
as Jerusalem, awesome as an army with banners!*
SONG OF SOLOMON 6:4 NKJV

In the ancient love poem of the Song of Solomon, the
king praises the beauty of his bride. Who doesn't love
to see a man adore his beloved? Perhaps today is your
wedding day, but probably not. Still, because He (the
Prince and Bridegroom of heaven) has set His love on
you, today is one to celebrate.

You are loved, adored, cherished.

Pharaoh's Daughter: Beauty under Pressure

A princess, one of Pharaoh's daughters, came down to bathe in the river, and as she and her maids were walking along the riverbank, she spied the little boat among the reeds and sent one of the maids to bring it to her. . . . She named him Moses (meaning "to draw out") because she had drawn him out of the water.

EXODUS 2:5, 10 TLB

She was pagan royalty, but she had compassion. She refused prejudice and used her power to save a life. Beauty is doing what is right.

Noah's Wife: Beauty in Loss

*So Noah, with his sons, his wife,
and his sons' wives, went into the ark
because of the waters of the flood.*

GENESIS 7:7 NKJV

She isn't named in scripture, but she shared a huge boat with her husband and family and multitudes of animals during the worst flood on the planet.

Did she realize she would lose everything that wasn't inside, that even the earth would look different when she emerged? Whether or not she was outwardly attractive, she must have been a raving beauty on the inside to submit and share and survive like she did.

Rahab: Beautified by Faith

By faith—because she believed in God and his power—Rahab the harlot did not die with all the others in her city when they refused to obey God, for she gave a friendly welcome to the spies.

HEBREWS 11:31 TLB

Rahab didn't have a beautiful profession. But she chose to believe in the God of Israel and risked her life to help His people. Her faith was counted to her for righteousness, and she was welcomed into the fold of God's chosen nation. She even became a link in the earthly lineage of Christ. Her faith beautified her.

Priscilla:
Beauty in Ministry

*When Aquila and Priscilla heard [Apollos],
they took him aside and explained to
him the way of God more accurately.*
ACTS 18:26 NKJV

*Priscilla and Aquila, my fellow workers in Christ
Jesus, who risked their own necks for my life,
to whom not only I give thanks, but also
all the churches of the Gentiles.*
ROMANS 16:3–4 NKJV

The ultimate ministry power couple—Priscilla and
Aquila. Together, they discipled the great evangelist
Apollos and were supports and fellow laborers with
the apostle Paul.

Not needing her own billing, Priscilla is beautiful
in her attitude and fervor.

Lydia: Beautiful in Hospitality

One of them was Lydia, a saleswoman from Thyatira, a merchant of purple cloth. She was already a worshiper of God and as she listened to us, the Lord opened her heart and she accepted all that Paul was saying. She was baptized along with all her household and asked us to be her guests. "If you agree that I am faithful to the Lord," she said, "come and stay at my home." And she urged us until we did.

ACTS 16:14–15 TLB

Creative hospitality may be a gift, but we can all exercise it a little. A home that is a sanctuary for the family and a haven for others is a blessing.

Be beautifully hospitable!

Jephthah's Daughter: Beautiful in Dedication

When Jephthah came to his house at Mizpah, there was his daughter, coming out to meet him with timbrels and dancing; and she was his only child. . . . So she said to him, "My father, if you have given your word to the LORD, do to me according to what has gone out of your mouth, because the LORD has avenged you of your enemies, the people of Ammon."

JUDGES 11:34, 36 NKJV

Jephthah's daughter insisted that he keep his vow and committed her life to service and celibacy for the rest of her days.

Keep your vows.

Martha: Beauty of Activity

Now it happened as they went that He entered a certain village; and a certain woman named Martha welcomed Him into her house.

LUKE 10:38 NKJV

Martha has gotten a bad rap in modern-day women's ministry. She is remembered as being the workaholic, nonrelational, frantic, probably first-born, older sister. And she did have a tendency to fret about things, or else Jesus wouldn't have reminded her that she didn't have to take on so much stress.

But Martha was a doer, and Jesus didn't want to stifle that but only guide it. Hers was a beauty of activity, which just needed His redirection.

Mary: Beauty in Listening

*And she had a sister called Mary, who also
sat at Jesus' feet and heard His word.*

LUKE 10:39 NKJV

Mary was pretty much the opposite of her sister Martha. Oh, she had goals and gifts, but she wasn't frantic about the details of life.

While none of us has the luxury of sitting and musing for the majority of our lives, Mary shows us how to act on good priorities. Her rule is "When Jesus is talking, stop and listen."

Today, be beautiful by how you soak up every word He is speaking to you.

BEAUTIFUL IN LOSS

Beautiful Findings

"Or if there is a woman who has ten silver coins, if she should lose one, won't she take a lamp and sweep and search the house from top to bottom until she finds it? And when she has found it, she calls her friends and neighbours together. 'Come and celebrate with me,' she says, 'for I have found that coin I lost.'"

LUKE 15:8–9 PHILLIPS

There is so much beauty in found things! From the simple—like car keys—to the sacred—like missing children! This woman had lost ten coins, valuable coins.

What have you lost?

Rely on God's sufficiency while you hope for the beauty of finding.

Worship in Your Tragedy

Then Job stood up and tore his robe in grief and fell down upon the ground before God. "I came naked from my mother's womb," he said, "and I shall have nothing when I die. The Lord gave me everything I had, and they were his to take away. Blessed be the name of the Lord." In all of this Job did not sin or revile God.

JOB 1:20–22 TLB

Have you suffered tragedy? Most of us have or will.

Like Job, you can call out to God, choosing the beauty of worship over the ugliness of blasphemy.

Just beyond Death

The pains of death surrounded me.
PSALM 116:3 NKJV

O death, where is thy sting?
O grave, where is thy victory?
1 CORINTHIANS 15:55 KJV

Death is our worst physical enemy. And it represents our even greater Enemy, Satan, who tries to lure us into spiritual death. There is not much beauty in the stark realities of corpses, caskets, and cemeteries. When death enters, beauty and hope run scared.

Well, not quite. Because Jesus conquered death, we can look death in the face and believe that beauty, eternal beauty, waits just beyond its threshold.

Divorced, but Not Destroyed

*"For the LORD God of Israel says that He hates
divorce, for it covers one's garment with
violence," says the LORD of hosts.*

MALACHI 2:16 NKJV

How can there be any beauty in the ravages of divorce?

There isn't—at least not in the mechanics and emotions of the ripping apart of a one-flesh relationship, the dismantling of a home. But there is beauty in the God who watches over and heals all those who take their shards of life to Him.

Today, God wants you to know that divorce doesn't have to destroy you.

Never More Abandoned

"Can a woman forget her nursing child, and not have compassion on the son of her womb? Surely they may forget, yet I will not forget you."

ISAIAH 49:15 NKJV

When my father and my mother forsake me, then the LORD will take care of me.

PSALM 27:10 NKJV

Foster care. Juvenile court. Child services.

All these phrases speak to the reality of lonely childhoods. The loss of parents (whether by tragedy or irresponsibility) is deep; it always follows the child into adult life.

Today, Jesus offers you the beauty of His beautiful, never-abandoning love.

Fountain of Renewed Youth

For You are my hope, O Lord GOD;
You are my trust from my youth.

PSALM 71:5 NKJV

Even though our outward man is perishing,
yet the inward man is being renewed day by day.

2 CORINTHIANS 4:16 NKJV

Lost innocence in childhood can never be regained. It is something that was never known, so often adults don't even realize their need to grieve it.

The God of heaven wants you to know that He can restore the beauty of youth even when it is past—maybe not in physical characteristics, but in the inner being, which He can continually renew.

Beautiful Strength

"We looked for peace, but no good came;
and for a time of health, and there was trouble!"

JEREMIAH 8:15 NKJV

*Therefore I take pleasure in infirmities,
in reproaches, in needs, in persecutions,
in distresses, for Christ's sake. For when
I am weak, then I am strong.*

2 CORINTHIANS 12:10 NKJV

Our bodies and souls are interconnected. One affects the other. The loss of health brings trauma to the spirit as well. But we must fight this downward spiral with the beautiful strength that comes from Christ. He makes even our weakness a triumph of His power.

Love Is the Way

*Bearing with one another, and forgiving one
another, if anyone has a complaint against
another; even as Christ forgave you, so you also
must do. But above all these things put
on love, which is the bond of perfection.*

COLOSSIANS 3:13–14 NKJV

Perhaps no emotional pain is quite as vivid as that of
a strained relationship. Whether a family tie, a friendship, or a marriage, fractured relationships are like a
vacuum in the soul, keeping us from truly being filled
with joy.

The Bible prescribes a way to manage strained
relationships.

Give love a chance to bring the beauty back.

All That Life Consumes

*To all who mourn in Israel he will give: beauty
for ashes; joy instead of mourning; praise instead
of heaviness. For God has planted them like
strong and graceful oaks for his own glory.*

ISAIAH 61:3 TLB

Think about what is left after a house fire. Charred remnants of a family's life. Blackened metal here and there. And lots of ash.

Often, the trials of life incinerate what we hold dear. All we can then do is bring to God our smoking, cindery bowls of ashes.

Today, remember that He is the God who replaces our ash urns with beauty.

Trifling Losses

*Better a little with reverence for God
than great treasure and trouble with it.*

PROVERBS 15:16 TLB

It doesn't have to be a big loss. A small one sometimes hurts, too. A favorite mug broken; a pair of shoes ruined; a childhood memento destroyed or lost. Everything we lose reminds us that we are not destined ultimately for this earth.

We who belong to God are bound for that other land, the place where nothing is ever lost and all the disappointments of this life will be swallowed up in an unspeakable beauty.

BEAUTIFUL IN NEED

Confidence in Him

For the LORD will be your confidence.
PROVERBS 3:26 NKJV

We have the idea that confidence makes us beautiful
and desirable. After all, the cover girl appears to never
have fears, suffer from anxiety, or experience insecurity.
But your Prince is drawn to your need. He is not put off
by the deep inhibitions you feel about yourself today.
He knows that it is His grace in you that gives you real
confidence. And He already knows the beauty in you.
Run to His strength today.

You Need Wisdom

*Getting wisdom is the most
important thing you can do!*
PROVERBS 4:7 TLB

*And if, in the process, any of you does not know how
to meet any particular problem he has only to ask
God—who gives generously to all men without making
them feel foolish or guilty—and he may be quite sure
that the necessary wisdom will be given him.*
JAMES 1:5 PHILLIPS

Ask your heavenly Father for wisdom. He is drawn to
your need. He is ready and waiting to share His resources
with you. Let the beauty of His wisdom be yours today.

His Hand on Yours

In all your ways know, recognize,
and acknowledge Him, and He will direct
and make straight and plain your paths.

PROVERBS 3:6 AMPC

Today, you need guidance. You aren't smart enough to counsel yourself. In the decisions you have to make and the people you need to touch, you need God's hand on yours, directing your every turn.

There is no personal beauty for the woman who tries to do it on her own. Acknowledge Him today.

A Peaceful Woman

*"Peace I leave with you, My peace I give to you;
not as the world gives do I give to you. Let not
your heart be troubled, neither let it be afraid."*

JOHN 14:27 NKJV

This world needs peace. Our homes need peace. Our souls need peace.

Jesus promised to leave us His very own peace, the kind that comes from knowing He is Lord over all and from trusting in His power to overcome whatever we face.

Perhaps there is nothing quite so lovely as a woman who is at peace with herself and her world.

Bring this need to Him today.

BEAUTIFUL FOR OTHERS

Think Others

*[Love] does not behave rudely, does not
seek its own, is not provoked, thinks no evil.*
1 CORINTHIANS 13:5 NKJV

*Let no one seek his own, but each
one the other's well-being.*
1 CORINTHIANS 10:24 NKJV

*Let each of you look out not only for his own
interests, but also for the interests of others.*
PHILIPPIANS 2:4 NKJV

If you are primarily interested in your own benefits and
well-being and promotion, then you do not know the
beautiful love Christ has for you.

Today, He wants you to receive His love and then
pass it on. Think *others*.

Action Love

Love suffers long and is kind; love does not envy;
love does not parade itself, is not puffed up.

1 CORINTHIANS 13:4 NKJV

The kind of love described in 1 Corinthians 13 is divine love, and it is beautiful. It is not primarily an emotion but an action. This was the love that moved the heart of God to send His Son to the world, the kind of love that millions have tested and proved and found strong and true.

Today, He calls us to show the beauty of this love to others.

It's Bearable

[Love] bears all things, believes all things.
1 CORINTHIANS 13:7 NKJV

*And be kind to one another,
tenderhearted, forgiving one another,
even as God in Christ forgave you.*
EPHESIANS 4:32 NKJV

Believe that God is at work in the lives of your brothers and sisters in Christ. Believe the best about them. When you do, there is beauty in you.

A cynical, critical, fault-finding spirit beautifies no one and certainly casts a shadow on Christ, whose name you bear.

Choose to go beyond—believe the best, be forgiving and supportive. It's beautiful.

Beautiful Burden Bearer

[Love] hopes all things, endures all things.
1 Corinthians 13:7 NKJV

Bear one another's burdens,
and so fulfill the law of Christ.
Galatians 6:2 NKJV

It's not fun to be inconvenienced, but it's part of being family, right? And it's part of being the family of God. We put up with one another's oddities and overlook some irritating traits. But then there are things that are more difficult to take; these we have to "bear" and "endure." Divine love gives us the power to do that.

Today, be a burden bearer and grow more beautiful in the process.

Bringing Beauty Home

These older women must train the younger women to live quietly, to love their husbands and their children, and to be sensible and clean minded, spending their time in their own homes, being kind and obedient to their husbands so that the Christian faith can't be spoken against by those who know them.

TITUS 2:4–5 TLB

It is a beautiful thing to grow in understanding.

God has ordained a mentoring program for women that brings older women and younger women together so that wisdom about establishing beauty in the home may be passed on.

How can you be part of this program? Look for a way.

For Your Own Family

Her children stand and bless her;
so does her husband.

PROVERBS 31:28 TLB

You are beautiful for your family. Women were designed by God to be the beauty bearers and beauty creators in the home. Your beauty is not for you to consume on your own interests but for you to use in nurturing your husband and children. What can you do today to make their lives more beautiful?

A Lamp for Others

She extends her hand to the poor, yes,
she reaches out her hands to the needy.

PROVERBS 31:20 NKJV

Men, broken from battle and suffering in primitive hospitals, called Florence Nightingale "the lady with the lamp." She was an angel of mercy, probably the most beautiful person they had ever seen because of her compassionate service to them.

In a world of self-focus, where there is disdain for the homeless, dirty, and traumatized, a woman who embodies a spirit of compassion is a beautiful creature indeed. God commends this kind of service as a trait of ultimate womanhood. Pick up your own lamp and get started.

Working for Others

She seeks wool and flax,
and willingly works with her hands.
PROVERBS 31:13 NKJV

I don't have a spinning wheel. I don't work with wool and flax. But I do have work that God has given me to do. So do you.

We are lovely when we are filling our place, willingly accepting the assignment given to us by the Creator of the universe. He has placed within us gifts and abilities. He expects us to discover and develop them. And if He opens the door to marriage and children, that is to be the major part of our responsibilities.

Be beautiful; work at it.

Love with Skin

*What I am eager for is that all the Christians
there will be filled with love that comes from
pure hearts, and that their minds will be
clean and their faith strong.*

1 Timothy 1:5 TLB

Working daily with others is a wonderful opportunity
to embody the beautiful spirit of Christ. Oh, I know
it seems humdrum and routine and some coworkers
can be irritating and downright ornery. But God has
arranged it so that we will have the opportunity to
rub elbows with those who need to see His love with
skin on.

How's the modeling going?

Salty, Bright Beauty

"You are the salt of the earth; but if the salt loves its flavor, how shall it be seasoned? It is then good for nothing but to be thrown out and trampled underfoot by men. You are the light of the world. A city that is set on a hill cannot be hidden."

MATTHEW 5:13–14 NKJV

In the frenzy of fashion and the confusion of gender, your joyful celebration of the woman God appointed you to be is a lovely declaration of truth to the culture. Be salt. Be light. Spread the delightful savor of His splendor, and shine brightly on everyone near you.

They're Everywhere!

For I am not ashamed of the gospel of Christ:
for it is the power of God unto salvation
to every one that believeth.

ROMANS 1:16 KJV

You know them. You see them at work, the gym, the grocery store, even in church. Scoffers may all begin their journeys because of a deep personal disappointment. Their feelings of resentment are not dealt with, and they develop a harsh view of anyone who would believe there is a God who cares.

Your beauty as a woman who shows the love of Christ in practical ways is a magnet to the truth.

Doing Good

She will do him good and not
evil all the days of her life.

PROVERBS 31:12 KJV

You are beautiful when you are doing good for those in your family.

Here the Bible is speaking specifically of wives and husbands, but the principle applies to everyone, and especially to those in our own families. The Bible never applauds looking out for self; it always approves looking to the needs of others.

Real beauty is giving, and when you give to others, whether it is time or compassion or another chance when they don't deserve it, you are stunning.

Not My Way

*"Where have you come from?" the Lord asked
Satan. "From earth, where I've been watching
everything that's going on," Satan replied.*

JOB 2:2 TLB

Do you think God has asked Satan about you like He
did about Job?

Your surrendered beauty is a statement to the devil
as well as to human beings. When you obey God's
commands and allow Him to shine through you, you
are correcting what Eve did wrong. You are proving
that a human woman chooses to be beautiful God's
way and not her own way.

Shine On!

"Let your light so shine before men,
that they may see your good works
and glorify your Father in heaven."

MATTHEW 5:16 NKJV

God wants you to do good deeds in public. Not to be praised, but to be a neon sign pointing to Him.

As a woman who has dedicated her life to Him, you are His ambassador, His salesgirl so to speak. You are representing Him with every outfit you wear and every attitude you take.

So take care with your wardrobe, smile a little brighter, and shine on!

BEAUTIFUL FOR HIM

He Chose You for Himself

*He chose us in Him before the foundation
of the world, that we should be holy and
without blame before Him in love.*

EPHESIANS 1:4 NKJV

You are not a random creation. And your redemption was not a coincidence. It was planned that you should be born and that you should be redeemed. God chose you.

Being chosen is a compliment; it means you are valuable. In the eyes of Christ, you are lovely and treasured. Let the thrill of that wash over you today, and spread it to those around you.

He Wanted You First

We love him, because he first loved us.
1 JOHN 4:19 KJV

Women like to be wooed and won. And men were designed to do the pursuing.

More than a beautiful gender distinction, this age-old drama actually reflects God's relationship with us. He saw us and wanted us. He made the first move—in creation—and then again in salvation. His eyes are always watching for us. He never tires of showing His love for us. The only way we can escape this incredible love is to run from Him. It is thrilling to be wanted by God.

The Warrior of Your Heart

*And he personally bore our sins in his own
body on the cross, so that we might be dead
to sin and be alive to all that is good.*

1 PETER 2:24 PHILLIPS

Christ died for us, giving up His life for ours.

In all the great romance tales, the warrior is willing
to die for the sake of the beautiful maiden he wants to
rescue. Jesus is that Warrior. He is not willing to let the
Enemy have us. He was willing to fight to the death for
us. What a love He has for you!

Beautifully Pure

[Jesus] gave Himself for us, that He might redeem us
from every lawless deed and purify for Himself His
own special people, zealous for good works.

TITUS 2:14 NKJV

I've never seen a bride who wasn't scrubbed and fresh
and radiant. There is something about a wedding day
that makes you take extra care. It's a day to be beautifully
clean.

Jesus knew that we could not cleanse ourselves, so
He redeemed us and purified us with His own blood.
All we have to do is receive that on our behalf. He has
provided all we need to be beautifully pure.

Beautiful and Special

For no one ever hated his own flesh,
but nourishes and cherishes it,
just as the Lord does the church.

EPHESIANS 5:29 NKJV

A man who loves his wife will take delight in making her more beautiful by giving her pretty clothing, buying her perfume and flowers, maybe giving her a day at the spa. This is a small reflection of the heart of God.

Jesus, our Bridegroom, nourishes us with His love and cherishes us in many ways. We are more beautiful when we look for the ways He is showing us that we are special to Him.

The Bride Price

*Knowing that you were not redeemed with
corruptible things, like silver or gold, from your
aimless conduct received by tradition from your
fathers, but with the precious blood of Christ,
as of a lamb without blemish and without spot.*

1 PETER 1:18–19 NKJV

In ancient Israel (and in some countries today), a bride
price must be paid to the family of the bride for the loss
of their daughter, showing how valuable the woman is
and how much the husband-to-be wants her.

Jesus paid the bride price for us with His own blood.
It cost Him everything. We can tell by that how much
we mean to Him.

Prepared Place

*In my Father's house are many mansions: if it were
not so, I would have told you. I go to prepare a
place for you. And if I go and prepare a place for
you, I will come again, and receive you unto myself;
that where I am, there ye may be also.*

JOHN 14:2–3 KJV

It isn't enough for the groom to love the bride; no, he
wants to spend his life in relationship with her, to live
with her in his house.

Jesus wants us to be with Him. He is getting things
ready for the big day.

Escape from the Tower

[The Father] has delivered and drawn us to Himself out of the control and the dominion of darkness and has transferred us into the kingdom of the Son of His love.

COLOSSIANS 1:13 AMPC

Don't ever forget that you had no chance of real love if Jesus had not come to die for you. Like the fairy-tale princess in the tower, you had no hope of escape.

Jesus came and rescued you from the dominion of darkness. And now, if you have received Him, you are living in the kingdom of love with Him.

He's Coming

*Looking for that blessed hope, and the
glorious appearing of the great God
and our Saviour Jesus Christ.*
TITUS 2:13 KJV

God will never forget us. He has loved too much, fought
too hard, paid too dear, and prepared too long. He is
coming, in the clouds, to get us. It will be a glorious
day when we stand in His presence. All the dust of earth
will have evaporated, and we will have donned our
new eternally beautiful bodies. What a day that will be!

BEAUTIFUL FOR WITNESS

An Image of His Glory

*But we all, with open face beholding as in
a glass the glory of the Lord, are changed
into the same image from glory to glory,
even as by the Spirit of the Lord.*

2 Corinthians 3:18 KJV

You, with all your redeemed and surrendered beauty
in Christ, are a witness to His glory.

All the fashion sense and fleeting trends of this world
are suddenly very temporary when one has a glimpse
of what it means to be loved by Him.

You are His image in the world.

Redeemed Statement

I will ransom them from the power of the grave;
I will redeem them from death.

HOSEA 13:14 KJV

If you belong to Christ, you have been redeemed from the very jaws of eternal death. And that is a powerful witness. Our world lives in fear. And with good reason. It is a very unsafe, unstable world. But we—who know the Lord of life and whom the grave no longer holds captive—are God's showcase.

Today, your trust in Him as you approach life with all its uncertainties is a beautiful statement of His redemption.

You Tell of His Plan

*It is he who saved us and chose us for his
holy work not because we deserved it
but because that was his plan long before
the world began—to show his love and
kindness to us through Christ.*

2 TIMOTHY 1:9 TLB

God planned for you to be His long ago. Before even
a cell of your body was present on this earth, you were
very present in His plan.

Through His Son, God reached out to us with love
and kindness. In this He offered us what no one else
could. And today, He is still working to bring that plan
to beautiful completion.

Nothing but Grace

Having predestined us to adoption as sons by Jesus Christ to Himself, according to the good pleasure of His will, to the praise of the glory of His grace, by which He made us accepted in the Beloved.

Ephesians 1:5–6 nkjv

God's grace, undeserved favor.

John Newton, slave trader turned song writer and preacher, understood the beauty of this. In the mighty words of his "Amazing Grace," Newton penned the witness that each of us can claim as our own: "How precious did that grace appear the hour I first believed."

Beautiful witness. Grace today; grace tomorrow; grace for eternity.

They Read You

For the invisible things of him from the creation of the world are clearly seen, being understood by the things that are made, even his eternal power and Godhead; so that they are without excuse.

ROMANS 1:20 KJV

No one is excused.

The most cultured. The most primitive.

Everyone has the world to view. And it tells of God's power in great detail.

They also have you. They can see the witness in your life. You are a living testimony to His power to bring beauty to a human life.

Let others read a clear testimony today.

The Witness of Kindness

She opens her mouth with wisdom,
and on her tongue is the law of kindness.

PROVERBS 31:26 NKJV

There is no beauty without kindness.

A razor-sharp tongue quickly destroys any attractiveness that would otherwise be seen. Cutting words and careless comments are the way to prove that there is no inner beauty of soul.

Jesus called us to love, to speak gentle words, to practice forgiveness and mercy. Women who make sure to guard their words are women who truly understand beauty.

Testament to His Greatness

Great is the LORD, and greatly to be praised; and his greatness is unsearchable.

PSALM 145:3 KJV

Every time you are Christlike in a situation where you would naturally be inclined otherwise is a witness to His greatness.

Being surrendered in actions and reactions and attitudes is a matter of daily choices to let the Spirit have control. This points to Him.

Those who do not know Him cannot help but follow their sinful tendencies. When you show them another way, they can see that it has to be Him in you. How beautiful!

You Are a Micro-Witness

And he is before all things,
and by him all things consist.

COLOSSIANS 1:17 KJV

There is nothing in this life that is not touched by God. He is the source; He is the energy; He is the constancy.

At times, matters of faith are seen as outdated and irrelevant to the modern discussion. Concepts like evolution seem to sidestep His relevance. But you are a witness that He is very present in your life and that because there is micro-involvement of the divine, there must also be macro-involvement of the same.

Thank you for proving it so beautifully.

You Are a Portrait

You can never please God without faith, without depending on him. Anyone who wants to come to God must believe that there is a God and that he rewards those who sincerely look for him.

HEBREWS 11:6 TLB

The very image of you, a human woman, committed to Christ and ordering your life in a way that points to His existence—you are another link in a glorious procession through the ages. Your portrait is in the gallery; the dissertation of your life has been cataloged. You tell the story well.

His Creativity in You

*When I consider Your heavens, the work of Your
fingers, the moon and the stars, which You have
ordained. What is man that You are mindful of him,
and the son of man that You visit him?*

PSALM 8:3–4 NKJV

Think how incredibly awesome it was of God to write
the witness of His glory in things that are visible!

The vast heavens, the celestial bodies—they all
blaze with the message of His creative presence.

You, with your God-given beauty and your grace-
filled life, are a witness to it as well.

Today, you are the star; shine!

BEAUTIFUL FOR ETERNITY

The Eternal, Inside Person

Rather let it be the hidden person of the heart, with the incorruptible beauty of a gentle and quiet spirit, which is very precious in the sight of God.

1 PETER 3:4 NKJV

When my children were little and we discussed death, I would tell them that the "inside person" went to be with Jesus.

The inner person is the one who is the most real. Under this fading body, if we have been saved by Him, is a spirit that has been touched with the loveliness of His grace. And its beauty will last for eternity.

Wrinkles No More

*Who will transform our lowly body that it
may be conformed to His glorious body,
according to the working by which He is able
even to subdue all things to Himself.*

PHILIPPIANS 3:21 NKJV

Wrinkles are a thing of earth. Yay! Add to that list all the warts and blemishes and bumps and lumps and diseases and disorders that make up the laundry list of human ailments, and you have what the apostle Paul called a "lowly body."

Today, rejoice in the knowledge that you will be beautiful for eternity—in a new body!

Tears Wiped Away

*And God shall wipe away all tears from their eyes;
and there shall be no more death, neither sorrow,
nor crying, neither shall there be any more pain:
for the former things are passed away.*

REVELATION 21:4 KJV

The ability to cry is a human gift. The body is capable of expressing what is going on inside, proving the interconnectedness of the physical and emotional parts of us.

Some tears are ones of joy; but mostly, tears denote sorrow. And God is going to eliminate sorrow from our eternal existence. Won't that be beautiful?

Eternal Wholeness

*And this is the testimony: that God has given
us eternal life, and this life is in His Son. He who
has the Son has life; he who does not have
the Son of God does not have life.*

1 John 5:11–12 NKJV

Do you feel good today? How do you know? Against
what standard are you judging it?

I wonder if we even really know how total wholeness
feels.

When we live eternally with God, we will have a new
measurement by which to judge. It will be a template
of beautiful, complete vitality.

No Beauty Sleep

The former things are passed away.

REVELATION 21:4 KJV

You need your "beauty sleep."

Heard anyone say that?

Yeah, they were right. Most of us do. But one of these days you will do it for the last time. You will take your last night's sleep, last midday nap, last snooze in the easy chair. And that's not morbid. It's quite wonderful.

In God's home, you won't need to rest. Your body and mind will be eternally energized. Not to mention that nothing could improve your out-of-this-world beauty.

Clear Vision;
Beautiful Revelations

For now we see through a glass, darkly;
but then face to face: now I know in part;
but then shall I know even as also I am known.

1 Corinthians 13:12 kjv

The best we can do down here is a smudgy reflection of God's glory. Our best youthful beauty is like peering into the tarnished silver of an antique mirror. It's not very clear.

But one day we will see Him face-to-face, and our eyes will be fully opened to see the majesty of that glory revealed in us as we never saw it on earth.

Radiant Reflection

*But we all, with unveiled face, beholding as
in a mirror the glory of the Lord, are being
transformed into the same image from glory
to glory, just as by the Spirit of the Lord.*

2 Corinthians 3:18 NKJV

Though our vision isn't what God can see, even our
earthly eyes can recognize that we are being transformed
a little more every day into a reflection of Him. Through
His grace, through our trials and testings, through our
faith, we are being conformed to His beautiful image.
Today, hold on to the radiant progress you see!

Fixed on That Day

*Surely goodness and mercy shall follow me
all the days of my life: and I will dwell
in the house of the LORD for ever.*

PSALM 23:6 KJV

In God's presence, we will see how He worked in us all along. We will delight in the knowledge that He led us all the way, that it was His hand that sculpted and fashioned us and His goodness and mercy that followed us.

Don't despair, no matter what you see today. Keep your eyes fixed on that day when you will forever be in His house.

Ever with Him

Verily I say unto you, I will drink no more of the fruit of the vine, until that day that I drink it new in the kingdom of God.
MARK 14:25 KJV

Blessed are they which are called unto the marriage supper of the Lamb.
REVELATION 19:9 KJV

So shall we ever be with the Lord.
1 THESSALONIANS 4:17 KJV

Much of the language of the Bible is romance/marriage language. We are going to spend happily-ever-after with our Prince, Jesus, glorified by His love and delighting in His presence.

No other beauty compares to that.